Audrey
A LIFE IN PICTURES

Audrey
A LIFE IN PICTURES

CAROL KRENZ

MetroBooks

MetroBooks

An Imprint of Friedman/Fairfax Publishers

© 2000, 1997 by Michael Friedman Publishing Group, Inc.

Library of Congress Cataloging-in-Publication Data

Krenz, Carol.
        Audrey Hepburn: a life in pictures/ Carol Krenz.
                        p.   cm.
        Includes bibliographical references, filmography, and index.
        ISBN 1-56799-531-4 (hc)
        1. Hepburn, Audrey, 1929–   —Portraits. I. Title.
PN2287.H43K74   1997
791.43'028'092—dc21
        [B]   97-8123
                                                                                CIP

Editor: Stephen Slaybaugh
Art Director: Kevin Ullrich
Designer: Millie Sensat
Photography Editor: Deidra Gorgos
Production Manager: Camille Lee

Color separations by Ocean Graphics International Company Ltd.
Printed in China by Leefung-Asco Printers

5   7   9   10   8   6

For bulk purchases and special sales, please contact:
Friedman/Fairfax Publishers
Attention: Sales Department
15 West 26th Street
New York, NY 10010
212/685-6610   FAX 212/685-1307

Visit our website: http://www.metrobooks.com

Dedication

For my husband, Gilbert, whose love makes all my

projects that much easier.

CONTENTS

Introduction

Above: In 1954 Audrey was one of the world's most visible stars. She had just won an Academy Award for her very first Hollywood film, *Roman Holiday*.

Opposite: In the 1950s Audrey's high sense of chic was apparent even in casual clothes. A turned up shirt cuff and a pair of earrings when combined with her graceful figure proved that sometimes less is more.

From the moment Audrey Hepburn greeted audiences in *Roman Holiday* (1953) as the regal Princess Anne, it was clear that this was no ordinary actress. Her angular face framed enormous almond-shaped eyes, her voice rose and fell like a child's lullaby, and her narrow figure floated with balletic grace. This was a star of great magnitude.

Who could have known that this engaging pixie with the sylphlike silhouette had suffered enormous deprivations while growing up hungry during World War II? Audrey was ebullient and radiant, sometimes a headstrong colt, often a small kitten. She was always unmistakably elegant and stylish—even in Capri pants and flat ballet slippers.

Forever a contradiction—both chic and waiflike—Audrey Hepburn conquered Hollywood during a period when peroxide blondes and large breasts were the white bread of the 1950s movie meal. Yet audiences happily welcomed Audrey's European style, her sweet intellect and bubbling champagne wit. She was compelling in her doe-eyed impishness. She blended a crooked smile with aristocratic posture. And her voice was forever melodious, resonating with surprise, wonder, and mischief.

Audrey often portrayed the ugly duckling who grows into a swan. To the French novelist Colette, she was the only Gigi worth consideration. In the play's 1951 Broadway run, she breathed youthful exuberance into the role of the innocent and gangly courtesan-in-training. For *Roman Holiday*, she played the princess looking for the comforts of the commoner's life. As the lovesick title character in *Sabrina* (1954), she blossomed from a plain Jane into a French-finished sophisticate.

In *My Fair Lady* (1964), she struck a familiar chord by assuming the role of a Cockney street urchin who is transformed into a lady. And as Holly Golightly, in the 1961 film of Truman Capote's *Breakfast at Tiffany's*, Audrey portrayed the high-toned hooker of haute couture.

Onscreen, Audrey Hepburn presented the world with an image of indelible poise, charm, and gay spontaneity. Both audiences and her leading men—who included such luminaries as Fred Astaire, Gregory Peck, Gary Cooper, and Cary Grant—adored her, and she seemed to adore them right back. And while she embodied all of these irresistible traits in reality, she was also plagued by insecurity, eating disorders, physical frailties, and painful self-doubt.

First, there was her lost childhood, which began with the scarring memories of her parents' divorce. Then came acute hunger, hardship, and illness in Holland during World War II. After the liberation of Holland, when life should have seemed so much sweeter, Audrey's dreams of becoming a prima ballerina—to which she had committed years of rigorous study—were dashed.

Undaunted, she persevered and detoured into theatrical reviews and ultimately films. Well into adulthood, a seemingly glamorous and privileged period of her life, she experienced personal anguish—two failed marriages, several miscarriages, and an overwhelming sense of fear and longing.

Through highs and lows that included Academy and Tony Awards, accidents, and injuries, Audrey remained fixed on family, duty, career, and simplicity of style and living. She froze like a deer in front of Hollywood's bright lights, favoring instead the tranquillity of Switzerland's quiet mountains and fresh air. She adored simple pleasures. She watched her two sons and her gardens grow.

Ultimately, it was her work for UNICEF as ambassador-at-large that brought her the most satisfaction. Devoting her final years to the plight of the world's starving children, she was concerned more for their health than for her own. Her untimely death in 1993 marked the departure of one of the most uniquely beautiful and altruistic people ever to grace the screen.

Opposite: For most portraits, Audrey preferred an earnest look rather than an open smile. She was extremely conscious of her crooked teeth.

Above: Audrey's dramatic jewel fashions in *Breakfast at Tiffany's* were the very thing she avoided in real life. Sparkle and flash were not important to her.

Chapter One

Into the Light

Above: Audrey at fourteen. Born Edda Hepburn in Brussels, Belgium, on May 4, 1929, Audrey was the daughter of Baroness Ella Van Heemstra of Holland and Joseph Hepburn-Ruston of England. Her father, an avowed Nazi sympathizer, was rumored to have embezzled some of his wife's funds. The couple divorced in 1935. Audrey spent time in England with her father after the divorce but was brought back to Arnhem in 1940. The baroness had reassurances from Queen Wilhelmina that Hitler would never invade Holland. The baroness had been misinformed.

Opposite: In this publicity still for *The Secret People*, Audrey poses in her dance costume, clearly demonstrating her natural regal bearing.

udrey with her mother in 1946. World War II had brought extreme hardship. Severe hunger reduced Audrey to a nervous, introverted, skinny child suffering from edema and hepatitis. At one point, Audrey said, she hid in a cellar without food for almost three weeks, thus sowing the seeds for future eating disorders. Whenever she felt hunger in future life, rather than giving in to it, she felt she had to "master" it. The Nazis seized the family estate and all goods by 1942. Audrey's escape was through her discipline and passion for ballet. She said that both she and her mother secretly raised funds for the Dutch Resistance.

Below: Audrey studied at the Arnhem Conservatory of Music and Dance during the war and later in England at the famed Notting Hill Gate School under Marie Rambert's direction. But it was soon obvious to Rambert that while Audrey was serious and dedicated, she lacked basic techniques and was too tall to be groomed into a professional dancer.

Above: Audrey's first break came at age seventeen. Because she was multilingual, she landed an appearance in a Dutch travelogue for KLM Airlines. Buoyed by this early success, Audrey and her mother settled in London after the war, gambling on a prospective film career for Audrey.

After some initial success in London theatrical revues, like *Sauce Tartare* and *Sauce Piquante*, Audrey began to be noticed. She landed small walk-on parts for Ealing Studios and Associated British Pictures. Here, she is shown in a scene from *Young Wives' Tales* (1951).

A udrey also caught the interested eye of Alec Guinness (left),
who quickly signed her for the small role of Chiquita in *The
Lavender Hill Mob* (1951), which also starred William Fox (right).

Audrey was being considered for a plum of a role in *The Secret People* (1951). While studio heads dragged their heels on final decisions, Audrey began dating James Hanson (shown here with Audrey in 1952), who was from a Yorkshire truck-building family. The baroness adamantly opposed the relationship, afraid that Audrey might settle into tweedy obscurity just as her career was about to take off. The couple announced their engagement anyway.

The difficult role of Nora in *The Secret People* challenged Audrey's burgeoning talents to the fullest. She played a young dancer caught up in the intrigue and anarchy of a terrorist group. In this scene, Audrey rehearses while actress Valentina Cortese looks on.

Above: While filming *Monte Carlo Baby* (1951) on location, Audrey caught the attention of French novelist Colette, who declared that Audrey was "a colt, unfinished, part woman, part boy, a virgin, perfection!" She cast Audrey as the title character in the Broadway play *Gigi*. Convincing Audrey to go to New York took some doing, but she finally agreed, much to the chagrin of fiancé James Hanson. Here, Audrey snuggles with Collette in Paris before sailing to New York for rehearsals.

Left: Audrey as the young Gigi. Writer Anita Loos and producer Gilbert Miller adored Audrey, although Miller was furious because Audrey had gained fifteen pounds (7kg) aboard the *Queen Mary* to New York, and he wanted her rail-thin. Audrey had to curb her never-ending passion for chocolate and was given strict orders to eat steak tartare and nothing else at Dinty Moore's. She lost the added weight plus an additional five pounds (2kg). Audrey had difficulty settling into the role and misbehaved until director Raymond Rouleau quickly straightened her out.

Left: Actress Cathleen Nesbitt, who played the role of Gigi's aunt, took Audrey under her wing and coached her in voice projection. *Gigi* opened to rave reviews on November 24, 1951. Critics found Audrey fresh and exuberant. Here, Audrey learns the fine art of being a courtesan from Nesbitt.

Right: After the initial run of *Gigi* but before the road tour began, Audrey flew to Rome to film *Roman Holiday*. Here is a last look at James Hanson as the couple arrive back in New York for her *Gigi* tour in 1952. Audrey broke off the engagement.

Chapter Two

The Hollywood Years

Above: When Gregory Peck began work with Audrey on *Roman Holiday* in the summer of 1952, he knew at once that all he'd be was a backdrop for her sparkling American debut. He insisted she get equal billing. She found him attractive and fatherly, while he adored her. They formed a lifetime friendship.

Opposite: *Roman Holiday* is a bittersweet story about putting duty and honor above one's personal happiness. Audiences gazing upon Audrey's majestic poise and gracious bearing sensed that these qualities were as natural to her as her ineffable charm.

Left: *Roman Holiday* was the first of several vehicles that allowed Audrey to act as both commoner and royal princess. Here, working in record-breaking heat in Rome during the summer of 1952, Audrey, as Princess Anne, enjoys an ice cream.

Right: Director William Wyler (right of the camera) had auditioned Audrey for the role of Princess Anne in *Roman Holiday* before she starred in *Gigi*. Positive that he had discovered a major motion picture star, he agreed to hold up production until Audrey was available. Wyler said that Audrey was "a princess, with so much poise—no doubt a result of her dancer's discipline and her mother's aristocratic background. But also, she was the spirit of youth." Here, she is seen with costar Gregory Peck.

The baroness and Audrey were reunited in New York on December 17, 1953, after a lengthy separation. Relations had always been strained but Audrey remained loving and dutiful.

Audrey won an Oscar for Best Actress for *Roman Holiday*. On March 25, 1954, she accepted the award from the much-revered Academy president, Jean Hersholt. After accepting the award, Audrey kissed him smack on the mouth, instead of the cheek, in childish excitement.

Above: Minutes after accepting her 1953 Oscar, Audrey realized that she'd misplaced it. Turning quickly on the steps of the Center Theater in New York, she raced back to the ladies' room, retrieved the award, and was ready to pose for photographers.

Right: Audrey poses with her Oscar for the press.

Left: Work on *Sabrina* began in the summer of 1953. As Sabrina Fairchild, the ugly duckling turned swan, Audrey played the chauffeur's daughter who falls in love with her father's wealthy playboy employers—first David, then his brother Linus. Left to right: Humphrey Bogart, Audrey, and William Holden.

Right: *Sabrina* brought French couturier Hubert de Givenchy into Audrey's life. As she wore "yards and yards" of his creations on the set, she never dreamed that he would be instrumental in creating the "Hepburn look." Audrey and Givenchy became friends for life and he remained her favorite designer. Here, wearing a famous Givenchy gown, Audrey takes direction from Billy Wilder.

Left: The newly sophisticated Sabrina (Audrey) has just returned from schooling in Paris, still nursing an unrequited love for David (William Holden). In this scene, David offers her a lift home, quite unaware of who she is.

Right: The onscreen romance between Sabrina Fairchild (Audrey) and Linus Larrabee (Humphrey Bogart) belied Bogart's utter contempt for her. He called Audrey a "rank amateur who needed a dozen takes." Bogart, fresh from *The Caine Mutiny* (1954), was brooding and abusive. He was shunned by both cast and crew.

William Holden fell in love with Audrey even before he met her and, according to him, stayed in love with her for the rest of his life. She was attracted to his charm and humor. They embarked on a doomed love affair. Holden suffered bouts of hypochondria and alcoholism. He was also married and a father. Beyond that, he'd had a vasectomy and Audrey wanted children more than anything. She ended the affair, and he never quite got over it.

Left: Audrey's idea of relaxation while living on her own was listening to music. She played records while she studied lines.

Right: Two instrumental directors in Audrey's life. Billy Wilder's (left) guidance led her to an Academy Award nomination for *Sabrina*. Once, in a moment of affection, he gave her a green bicycle, which she used to pedal around on the set. And William Wyler (right) has said that "she brought tears to [his] eyes."

Below: In August 1953, Audrey, sporting a pixie haircut, attended the London premiere of *Roman Holiday* in the company of songwriters Cole Porter (left) and Irving Berlin (right).

Above: After production on *Sabrina* wrapped up in August 1953, Audrey flew to London to attend the premiere of *Roman Holiday*. Friend Gregory Peck threw a party and writer/actor/director Mel Ferrer (pictured) was in attendance. The attraction between Audrey and Mel was immediate. He was handsome, moody, multitalented, and ambitious—and eleven years her senior. Married thrice before, he presented Audrey with a fatherly image.

Mel Ferrer proposed that they do the play *Ondine* by Jean Giraudoux. Audrey was delighted and together they starred on Broadway through the winter of 1953–1954. Notable critic Brooks Atkinson said *Ondine* was "ideal from every point of view—literature, acting, theater." As of Hepburn, he remarked, "She is tremulously lovely." Audrey won a Tony Award for her performance as the water sprite.

*O*ndine attracted celebrities and dignitaries. Here, some of the members of Ethiopian emperor Haile Salassie's immediate family visit with Mel and Audrey in Mel's dressing room.

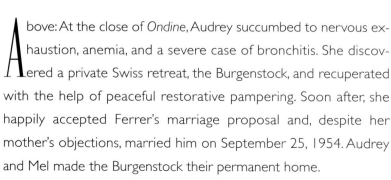

Opposite: Newlyweds Mel and Audrey duck reporters as they head to their Italian honeymoon villa.

Above: At the close of *Ondine*, Audrey succumbed to nervous exhaustion, anemia, and a severe case of bronchitis. She discovered a private Swiss retreat, the Burgenstock, and recuperated with the help of peaceful restorative pampering. Soon after, she happily accepted Ferrer's marriage proposal and, despite her mother's objections, married him on September 25, 1954. Audrey and Mel made the Burgenstock their permanent home.

Below: In October 1954 Audrey was pregnant, but suffered a miscarriage. Despite her tremendous disappointment, her sense of duty prompted her to keep working: Dino de Laurentiis was producing Leo Tolstoy's *War and Peace,* starring Audrey and Mel. *War and Peace,* (1956), directed by King Vidor, also starred Henry Fonda, Vittorio Gassman, May Britt, Arlene Dahl, Herbert Lom, John Mills, Barry Jones, and Oscar Homolka.

Left: Mel and Audrey arrive in Rome for preproduction on *War and Peace* in July 1955. Audrey had grown reclusive, nervous, and self-critical. She relied on Mel for everything. She hated her nostrils, her crooked teeth, and her skinny neck, and controlled all photos and costume fittings.

Right: Audrey, preparing for the role of Natasha Rostova in *War and Peace*, learns the Gavotte, an old French dance popular at the courts of Russian czars.

Below: While on the set of *War and Peace*, Audrey and Lea Seidel, who played Countess Rostova, greet Margaret Truman, daughter of former U.S. president Harry Truman.

Right: Kay Thompson, Fred Astaire, and Audrey (left to right) used Paris as a playground for the slightly satiric film about the fashion industry. Directed by Stanley Donen, *Funny Face* allowed Audrey to express the playful gamine aspects of her nature while at the same time emphasizing her incredible sense of style.

Above: A picture of grace in Astaire's arms, Audrey said, "I experienced the thrill that all women at some point in their lives have dreamed of—to dance just once with Fred Astaire."

Left: *Love in the Afternoon* (1957), directed by Billy Wilder, flew into production immediately after *Funny Face*, leaving little time for Audrey to rest. The film teamed her with the talents of Gary Cooper (left) and Maurice Chevalier (right).

Below: As worried as ever about what she considered to be an unattractive face, Audrey insisted that she approve her own stills, afraid that the cameraman might shoot her nostrils badly.

Left: Filming in Paris once again, Audrey spends time relaxing on a private estate with her mother.

Below: Audrey liked Gary Cooper and handled the often reserved Maurice Chevalier (pictured) with affection. It was rumored that they had an affair, but to say that Chevalier nursed a passionate fantasy about Audrey would probably be closer to the truth.

The only low points during the filming of *Love in the Afternoon* occurred when Mel interfered with Audrey's direction. The high point was the gift he gave her—a little Yorkshire terrier, Mr. Famous. Famous, as he was most often called, became Audrey's substitute child.

Right: The making of *The Nun's Story* (1959) was an intense but satisfying change of pace for Audrey. Two years in production, the drama follows the experiences of a young Belgian nun working among lepers in the Belgian Congo (now Zaire). Here, Audrey chats with author Kathryn Hulme while director Fred Zinnemann looks on.

Left: The majority of the filming for *The Nun's Story* took place in the heat of Stanleyville in the Belgian Congo. Dame Peggy Ashcroft eventually succumbed to the oppressive weather, but Audrey withstood it. She enjoyed Africa and didn't get sick until she arrived in Rome for more shooting. A severe case of kidney stones landed her flat on her back, and she panicked at the delays. She was already committed to doing another film under Mel's direction.

*T*he *Nun's Story* starred Audrey, Dame Peggy Ashcroft, and Peter Finch. Audrey was nominated again for an Oscar—she lost to Simone Signoret in *Room at the Top*—but she won the 1959 New York Film Critics' Award.

Opposite: Having enjoyed Fred Zinnemann's fine sense of direction and discipline on *The Nun's Story*, Audrey eagerly saluted him years later when she and Rosalind Russell congratulated Zinnemann on winning the Best Director and Best Picture Awards for *A Man for All Seasons* in 1967.

Right: Playing the rather strange and unearthly forest girl Rima in *Green Mansions* (1959) opposite Anthony Perkins, Audrey's every nuance was carefully orchestrated by husband/director Mel Ferrer. The actual shooting took place in Los Angeles. Other members of the cast included Henry Silva, Sessue Hayakawa, Lee J. Cobb, and Nehemiah Persoff.

Left: While it was artistic and beautiful to look at, *Green Mansions* seemed rather intellectual and remote, and did not have a broad audience appeal despite the fact that Audrey was stunning in new wide-screen CinemaScope.

A portrait of Audrey taken at the time of *Green Mansions*, in the late 1950s.

Below: In the spring of 1959, Audrey, Mel, and Famous flew from their home in Burgenstock, Switzerland, to Mexico. Audrey was to begin work on *The Unforgiven* (1960), directed by John Huston. The Mexican location served as a substitute for the Texas panhandle, which was too built up for the movie's time period.

Above: Because a fawn was central to the filming of *Green Mansions*, it was suggested that Audrey "adopt" one and slowly bond with it. Audrey raised Ip like her own child, bottle-feeding him every two hours. Ip soon became as much a part of the family as her Yorkie, Famous.

ight: *The Unforgiven* starred Audrey, Burt Lancaster (pictured), Audie Murphy, and Lillian Gish. Director John Huston earned everyone's respect because he encouraged his actors to take charge of their own roles. Wanting to please him, they always turned in exceptional performances.

eft: Audrey's favorite cameraman, Franz Planer, captured her amid the dust and grit of Mexican winds in *The Unforgiven*. Audrey was pregnant again and Mel didn't want her to do the film. She persisted anyway.

Left: As usual, Audrey got along with everyone on the set. But Lillian Gish (pictured here with Audrey) detested Audie Murphy, and it was rumored that Murphy was involved in nefarious cattle-rustling practices, comfortably protected by Hollywood's adulation of him.

Right: While shooting *The Unforgiven*, Audrey was thrown by a horse, aptly named Diablo. Wanting to appease Huston, she had agreed to the brief ride though she was terrified of horses. She broke several vertebrae and had to be flown to Los Angeles to recuperate for three weeks. She finished the film in a back brace. Here, she rests and knits between takes. Not long after the picture wrapped, Audrey miscarried yet again. She blamed herself and Mel blamed Huston.

Left: In this opening scene in front of Tiffany Jewelers in New York, audiences met Holly Golightly for the first time. Pondering the riches of her favorite haunt, Holly drinks coffee from a paper cup and nibbles a Danish in the wee small hours after a date. Audrey hated Danish and found it a difficult scene to swallow.

Below: Truman Capote wrote the part of Holly Golightly, a hooker who toys with the idea of bisexuality, for Marilyn Monroe. While he may not have been thrilled with Hepburn's sanitized portrayal, audiences and most critics were captivated by her poignant, waifish interpretation. Audrey, herself riddled with doubt, took the part as an opportunity to stretch her talents beyond the role of ingenue. Here, she is shown with costar George Peppard and the famous "Cat," whose real name was Rhubarb.

Directed by Blake Edwards and with an Oscar-winning musical score by Henry Mancini and costumes by Givenchy, *Breakfast at Tiffany's* provided Audrey with a pivotal moment, and a new sense of sophistication, in her career. In this final scene, Audrey, as Holly, has just angrily tossed Cat out a taxi window and then rescued him. She later confided that it was one of the most distasteful things she ever had to do.

Above: Audrey's next picture was yet another stretch, an opportunity to play against her image. This time the subject matter was deadly serious. Based on Lillian Hellman's play, *The Children's Hour* (1962) tells the story of two women friends who successfully run a private school for girls until one troubled student accuses them of lesbianism in a dramatic complaint to her powerful grandmother. Despite their denials, they are not believed and the door to tragedy opens.

Audrey decided to make the film because her friend William Wyler (*Roman Holiday*) was directing and because she wanted to work with Shirley MacLaine. Pictured are Audrey as Karen Wright and Shirley as the long-suffering Martha Dobie.

Right: In *The Children's Hour*, James Garner (pictured) plays Karen's fiancé, Dr. Joe Cardin, who ultimately breaks their engagement. *The Children's Hour* was a box-office bust but received Academy Award nominations. Not too long afterward, Audrey's pet terrier, Famous, got loose in traffic and was killed. Mel tried to soothe the inconsolable Audrey by presenting her with another Yorkie, Assam of Assam.

Early in 1962, Audrey accepted the role of Gabriel Simpson in *Paris When It Sizzles* (1964). Quelling any of her personal apprehensions, director Richard Quine presented the film to her as a chance for a comedic lark. On the surface, the film seemed ideal: Paris locations, Givenchy fashions, and breezy romantic comedy by George Axelrod. However, Audrey's misgivings about playing opposite William Holden after a nine-year separation were justified.

Left: Although Audrey was warm and affectionate with Holden, she couldn't bear his continued obsession for her. His drinking had become out of control, making the entire filming experience tense and worrisome.

Paris When It Sizzles, for all its visual beauty, landed with a thud at the critics' doorsteps. And during the final days of the filming, Audrey received news that the chalet at Burgenstock had been burglarized.

Right: Within days of completing *Paris When It Sizzles*, Audrey went into production on *Charade* (1963), an inspired pairing with the dapper Cary Grant (pictured). Directed by Stanley Donen, who had worked with Audrey on *Funny Face*, *Charade* is a tightly paced, witty, romantic comedy/thriller and is still considered one of the best of its genre.

Below: Grant, at age fifty-nine, conscious of the fact that Audrey was only thirty-three, welcomed a script that exploited their age differences by allowing his character to playfully fend off Reggie's romantic advances. Here, Audrey, as Reggie, tends to Grant's nasty cut, compliments of killer George Kennedy. The stellar cast also included James Coburn, Ned Glass, and Walter Matthau.

Above: Stylishly dressed in Givenchy, Audrey loved the role of Regina (Reggie) Lampert, who was cool, unflappable, resourceful, and poised—the complete antithesis to Audrey at the time, who had grown edgier than usual, nervous, obsessive, and fearful of kidnapping plots against her son, Sean. She'd work frantically for three weeks, fall apart, then throw herself back into another work frenzy for three more weeks.

Mel, Sean, and Audrey take a stroll in Paris while Audrey is on location for *Charade*. Rumors of Mel's occasional dalliances, albeit discreet ones, had reached Audrey. The couple were constantly at odds and then "patching things up." Audrey, herself a child of divorce, wanted a happy family life more than anything she could have professionally.

My Fair Lady was a visual feast and triumph of a film for movie-goers, although it handed Audrey a personal defeat. The musical production on Broadway, drawn from George Bernard Shaw's play *Pygmalion*, with music and lyrics by Alan Jay Lerner and Frederick Loewe, introduced the immortal characters of Professor Henry Higgins and Eliza Doolittle to packed houses in the late 1950s. Higgins and Doolittle were brought to life by Rex Harrison and Julie Andrews. Producer Jack Warner, however, wanted neither for his movie, preferring big box-office stars instead. Ultimately, he settled for Rex Harrison only after Cary Grant and Peter O'Toole turned him down. Audrey, who longed to play Eliza Doolittle, got her wish for a cool $1 million. But Alan Jay Lerner, among many in Hollywood, was shattered by Warner's decision to snub Julie Andrews. Here, Wilfrid Hyde-White, Harrison, and Audrey joke with the crew between takes. The film was directed by the legendary George Cukor.

Left: Audrey spent grueling months in preproduction for *My Fair Lady* learning Cockney dialogue, but she admitted years later that in the first half of the film, she was unconvincing as the poor little street urchin who becomes the valuable pawn in a wager between Professor Henry Higgins and Colonel Pickering. Higgins bet that he could take this lowly guttersnipe of a flower girl and pass her off as royalty within six months.

Above: Here, flower girl Eliza Doolittle has a few choice words for her father, Alfred (Stanley Holloway). The final cast included Wilfrid Hyde-White, Gladys Cooper, Mona Washbourne, Jeremy Brett, and Theodore Bikel.

As Eliza is "tested" part of the way through her metamorphosis into a lady, she is taken by Pickering and Higgins to Ascot Races. Here, we see a magnificent example of Sir Cecil Beaton's costume design. From left to right: Brett as Freddie Eynsford-Hill, Audrey as Eliza, Harrison as Higgins, and Hyde-White as Pickering.

This famous shot of Audrey preparing to leave for the Embassy ball demonstrates how she shone as the regal butterfly, Eliza, who unknowingly is quite prepared to help Professor Higgins win his bet.

The onscreen Eliza is depressed and fearful after the ball, mirroring what Audrey herself felt. She had been assured by Jack Warner that all her months of voice and singing lessons coupled with the prerecordings of her musical numbers would only have to be "enhanced" in certain spots. However, Warner never intended to use Audrey's singing voice at all—he planned to dub over her vocals with Marni Nixon's voice. When Warner sent an underling to break the news to Audrey, she stormed off the set, but returned and apologized the next day. When Hollywood learned that Audrey's voice had been dubbed, resentment mounted against her.

Left: Audrey attended the Oscars ceremony anyway, despite the fact that she had been snubbed by the Academy. Here, Audrey arrives with her mother, while Mel, suffering hurt pride, refused to attend.

Below: It was Audrey who announced in a genuinely delighted voice that the winner for Best Actor was none other than Rex Harrison. In fact, *My Fair Lady* took seven awards, including Best Director, Best Costume Design, and Best Picture.

Below: After a year off, during which time the family moved from the Burgenstock to Tolochenaz overlooking Lake Geneva, Audrey returned to Paris to work with director William Wyler on *How to Steal a Million* (1966) with Peter O'Toole.

Above: Ironically, Julie Andrews won the Best Actress category ostensibly for her role as Mary Poppins, but everyone knew this was the Academy's way of trying to acknowledge the rightful Eliza Doolittle. Here, Audrey poses good-naturedly with Julie. Regardless of the personal hurt Audrey must have felt, she was always gracious.

Right: *How to Steal a Million* was rather superficial fun, and certainly O'Toole enjoyed Audrey's company. Rumors surfaced that Audrey and O'Toole were having an affair, but since Audrey was still desperately trying to save her marriage and redecorating a new home, it seems unlikely.

Left: Audrey suffered another miscarriage and was eager to throw herself into some meaningful work. *Two for the Road* (1967) was just what the doctor ordered. A complete change of pace, it gave audiences a glimpse into a private side of Audrey not seen before. Directed by Stanley Donen, *Two for the Road's* sparkling script revealed a witty sophistication and refreshing candor. Costar Albert Finney (pictured) was like a breath of fresh air. The film also starred Eleanor Bron, William Daniels, Claude Dauphin, and Nadia Gray.

Opposite: *Wait Until Dark* (1967) was a thriller produced by Mel Ferrer and directed by Terence Young. It was a tour de force for Audrey, who played a young blind housewife terrorized by a psychotic killer looking for heroin. The film starred Efrem Zimbalist, Jr., Alan Arkin (pictured), Richard Crenna, and Jack Weston.

There was constant dissent on the set mostly due to the wrangling between Mel and Audrey. Tension was unbearable. Audrey, suffering a bout of anorexia, weighed only ninety-seven pounds (44kg). She missed being away from Sean and was keenly aware of Mel's "auditioning" of young actresses for one of his upcoming film projects. By the summer of 1967, after yet another miscarriage, Audrey had to accept that her marriage was finally over.

eft: Everything about *Two for the Road* was new for Audrey. Instead of Givenchy, she wore Mary Quant and Paco Rabanne. For once, Mel was not with her. She felt free and spontaneous, and Albert Finney recalled that he had never had a closer relationship with anyone than the one he'd had with Audrey on this film. The two were in a constant state of giggles on the set. Appropriately enough to Audrey's life, the film's plot centered on a couple's disintegrating marriage and their attempts to save it.

Chapter Three

The Italian Housewife

Above: In the summer of 1968, Audrey met the dazzling Dr. Andrea Dotti while on a Greek cruise. He was a prominent psychiatrist from a well-established Italian family. Despite religious and age differences (Dotti was thirty and Audrey forty), the couple married in a charming ceremony in Switzerland on January 18, 1969.

Opposite: Audrey posed for this shot in 1967, the year her marriage to Mel Ferrer ended.

Turning away from the Hollywood spotlight, Audrey renewed her health and spirit by retreating for a time to Switzerland. She busied herself with Sean, her gardens, and her close friends. One of Audrey's dearest friends was Doris Brynner (wife of actor Yul Brynner), pictured here with Audrey in 1968.

Above: Audrey and Andrea share an umbrella during a stroll a couple of months after the wedding. The couple settled in a large, airy apartment in Rome.

Below: Son Luca Dotti was born February 8, 1970. Audrey, worried that she might miscarry, had spent her lying-in period at Tolochenaz away from Andrea. It wasn't long, however, before rumors of affairs and photos in local scandal sheets reached her. Putting them aside, Audrey returned to Rome to renew her domestic role. She was still determined to put family first. Here she is Christmas shopping in relative peace in 1970.

At the theater in Rome in 1974: Audrey, with Sean and Andrea. Close friends observed that Andrea was using Audrey. When he needed a wife, she was supposed to be there, but when he caroused, he wanted her to "get scarce."

Left: After a seven-year absence from Hollywood, Audrey returned. She had turned down scripts for *Nicholas & Alexandra* and *40 Carats* because she wanted simply to be a wife and mother. Then, she agreed to star in *Robin and Marian* (1976) with Sean Connery.

Right: Audrey and director Richard Lester on the set of *Robin and Marian* in Pamplona, Spain. The studio system was gone, and working conditions were harder than what Audrey was used to. She developed dysentery and was ill for much of the shooting. The film did not turn out as she had envisioned it, but she promoted it nevertheless.

Left: Audrey's marriage was on the wane by the late seventies. There had been an attempted kidnapping of Dotti, rumors of his numerous affairs had become very public, and Audrey had suffered yet another miscarriage. Seen here with son Luca in Gstaad in 1979, Audrey's unhappiness is most apparent.

Below: Suppressing hurt, humiliation, and anger, Audrey sought escape in more work. This time, she starred in Sidney Sheldon's *Bloodline* (1979), receiving a million dollars plus a percentage of the film's receipts. While purists decried her choice of film, feeling it was not worthy of her talent, Audrey consoled herself in the company of actor Ben Gazzara.

Above: With Ben Gazzara in *Bloodline*. Finding a great deal of sympathy in Gazzara, Audrey said of him, "He was a lifesaver without even knowing it." Audrey claimed that it was Gazzara who helped her come to terms with her failed marriage. Later, she starred with him again in Peter Bogdanovich's film *They All Laughed* (1981).

Right: Happier times in 1979: Audrey with son Sean Ferrer at an art exhibition in New York.

Chapter Four

UNICEF and Beyond

Above: In 1980, a breath of fresh air walked into Audrey's life. He was Dutch-born Robert Wolders, the recent widower of actress Merle Oberon. With Wolders, Audrey bloomed and remained radiant. Audrey and Dotti were divorced in 1982, and Wolders and Audrey became inseparable.

Opposite: Resplendent as always in Givenchy creations, here is Audrey with Hubert de Givenchy at a retrospective in Tokyo in 1983.

Left: Audrey with Robert Wolders in 1988 at a tribute to actor Gregory Peck.

Right: In 1988, Audrey was invited to become a special Goodwill Ambassador for UNICEF. Here, she accepts the nomination. At age sixty, she found herself traveling more often than in all the years she had made films. Audrey's trips took her to Bangladesh, the Sudan, Ethiopia, El Salvador, Vietnam, and Somalia.

Above: One of her first stops for UNICEF was in Ethiopia. During this trip, Audrey was particularly concerned with obtaining vitamins for preventing blindness in children.

Above: Audrey with a young Ethiopian child in 1988. Audrey, who had suffered all her life trying to have a family, felt very emotional toward the plight of the world's children. "To save a million children is a God-given opportunity," she said.

R ight: Audrey visits with children in a slum area of Bangkok, Thailand.

L eft: Audrey took time out from her UNICEF duties to work with Steven Spielberg on *Always* (1989), which starred Richard Dreyfuss. Audrey played Hap, an angel who gently advises Dreyfuss on matters of the heart. It was a brief and luminous cameo role for Audrey, and her last film.

Left: Early in 1990, Audrey was presented with the 1989 Cecil B. DeMille Award for outstanding contribution to the field of entertainment.

Below: Audrey takes tea with First Lady Barbara Bush in 1990. UNICEF was one of the main topics of conversation. In 1992, President George Bush awarded Audrey the Presidential Medal of Freedom, but by that time she was too ill with cancer to attend the ceremonies.

Above: On February 19, 1991, former president Jimmy Carter presented Audrey with the 1990 Child Survival Award for her work and world travels as UNICEF Goodwill Ambassador.

Right: A glowing Audrey is happy to attend the 1991 Paris show for Givenchy's couture collections.

Left: Hubert de Givenchy and Audrey share a warm moment at the 1991 Paris show. Their careers had been intertwined since 1954.

Below: Taking time out from her continued work for UNICEF, Audrey filmed the PBS special "Gardens of the World." In July 1992, Audrey presented Sean Connery with the American Cinematheque Award for his film achievements.

Above: In November 1992, Audrey was diagnosed with colon cancer. She died on January 20, 1993, at the age of sixty-three. She had ignored the abdominal pain she had experienced on her last UNICEF trip to Somalia earlier in 1992—until it was finally too late.

Hepburn was buried at her Swiss country home, La Paisible, in a simple ceremony. Pallbearers included her sons, Sean and Luca, Hubert de Givenchy, Robert Wolders, Dr. Andrea Dotti, and Audrey's half-brother, Ian van Ufford. Mel Ferrer, seventy-five, was visibly grief-stricken and too frail to act as a pallbearer.

Right: Sons Sean Ferrer (left) and Luca Dotti at Audrey's funeral, on January 24, 1993. Sean said, "Mother believed in love—that it could heal, fix, mend, and make everything all right in the end."

Conclusion

The wonderful gossipy things that make actors' lives so much fun to read and talk about rarely come up in any discussions of Audrey Hepburn. In a way, this is a biographer's nightmare; in another way, it is a tribute to her honesty and simplicity.

Elizabeth Taylor said of Audrey at her death, "God has a most beautiful new angel now, that will know just what to do in heaven."

In life, happiness often eluded Audrey Hepburn. Much of her appeal derived from the aura of vulnerability that she exuded. Fun-loving and sad at the same time, she inspired devotion in her audiences.

Audrey's impeccable sense of style drew accolades throughout her career. Never less than elegant, no matter what her situation, Audrey was the image of poise. Perhaps what we didn't see was that Audrey took everything to heart. Her joy was serious, her

happiness was private, her anguish often hidden.

And so what Audrey Hepburn really left as her legacy was a timeless beauty and simplicity, and the example of a woman who placed family, honor, and duty, before all else.

Friends, actors, directors, lovers, and husbands—all who knew and loved her—had never an unkind word to say about her.

In the end, it was not the high fashion and the brilliant scripts, nor the peace and tranquillity of her marvellous Swiss retreat that brought her so much joy. It was the knowledge that she could alleviate children's suffering. Her work with UNICEF is what ultimately gave her life the meaning and depth she so desperately sought. That she died in the act of giving is what will be remembered long after the lights of Hollywood fade away.

And so Elizabeth Taylor is quite right. God indeed has a most beautiful new angel.

O pposite: Audrey wore numerous hats and headdresses throughout her career. The simplest were always the most dramatic.

B elow: Audrey at the 1986 Academy Awards in Los Angeles. Even
in middle age she set the standard for grace and beauty.

Filmography

One Wild Oat. Eros-Coronet: 1951.

Young Wives' Tale. Associated British: 1951.

Laughter In Paradise. Associated British: 1951.

The Lavender Hill Mob. Ealing: 1951.

Monte Carlo Baby. Ventura-Filmakers: 1952.

The Secret People. Ealing: 1952.

Roman Holiday. Paramount: 1953.

Sabrina. Paramount: 1954.

War and Peace. Ponti-De Laurentiis/Paramount: 1956.

Funny Face. Paramount: 1957.

Love in the Afternoon. Allied Artists: 1957.

Green Mansions. MGM: 1959.

The Nun's Story. Warner Bros.: 1959.

The Unforgiven. United Artists: 1960.

Breakfast at Tiffany's. Paramount: 1961.

The Children's Hour. Mirisch/United Artists: 1962.

Charade. Universal: 1963.

Paris When it Sizzles. Paramount: 1964.

My Fair Lady. Warner Bros.: 1964.

How to Steal a Million. Twentieth Century Fox: 1966.

Two for the Road. Twentieth Century Fox: 1967.

Wait Until Dark. Warner Bros.: 1967.

Robin and Marian. Columbia: 1976.

Bloodline. Paramount: 1979.

They All Laughed. Moon: 1981.

Always. Universal/United Artists: 1989.

Bibliography

Harris, Warren G. *Audrey Hepburn.* New York: Simon & Schuster, 1994.

Higham, Charles. *Audrey: The Life of Audrey Hepburn.* New York: Macmillan, 1986.

Karney, Robyn. *A Star Danced: The Life of Audrey Hepburn.* London: Bloomsbury, 1994.

Maychick, Diana. *Audrey Hepburn: An Intimate Portrait.* New York: Birch Lane Press, 1993.

Various. "A Tribute To Audrey Hepburn." *People.* Winter, 1993.

Photography Credits

Index